# Microcomputer
## Troubleshooting & Repair